I've Been
Where I'm Going

Praise for *I've Been Where I'm Going*

"Travel with Earnell Brown as she interprets and shares with us enchanting insights into her life journey ~ thusfar. Celebratory, honest, moving, deep, funny, fierce, uninhibited and always personal. And...you might see you!"
~ Jodi Yeldell, Ed.D & Doctor of Fabulosity

"*I've Been Where I'm Going* is an eloquent depiction of the soulful and imaginative reflections of a woman who embraces life and adventure!"
–Pearl Richardson Smith, Ph.D.

"Earnell Brown is a woman always on the move. This book of poetry is a passport to her world. Brown's work is filled with life lessons and personal reflections. At times she writes like a woman who has moved beyond the blues. After reading her poems one might be inspired to sing *Precious Lord*."
— E. Ethelbert Miller, Director of the African American Resource Center at Howard University

"The recurring theme of Earnell's beautiful, lyrical poetry is life. Her gift is the ability to translate life into words. Read and savor every page of *I've Been Where I'm Going*. You'll experience both the act and the art of living in all its beauty, humor, pain and most of all, its sheer joy."
— Niambi Brown Davis, author of *From Dusk to Dawn* and *Sanctuary*

"*I've Been Where I'm Going* is a revelation of Earnell's loving soul, beautiful spirit and faithful heart. Readers will be inspired to step out of life's boxes to enlarge their territories naturally and spiritually as they follow her through this wonderful journey of poetry."
— Dr. Lonise P. Bias, Motivational Speaker, Trainer, Consultant, Family and Teen Life Coach, and author

I've Been
Where I'm Going

Earnell Brown

TRAVELERSTREE
PUBLISHING
COMPANY

TravelersTree Publishing Company
P.O. Box 56756
Washington, DC 20040

ISBN: 9780982843000

Library of Congress Control Number: 2010931367

Adinkra symbol meaning BI NKA BI "Peace and Harmony"

Cover and Interior Designed by The Writer's Assistant
www.thewritersassistant.com

Cover Photograph of the Grenadines, West Indies by Earnell Brown

Paintings by Earnell Brown on pages 24, 38, 65

Photographs by Earnell Brown appear on pages

27, Jamaica, West Indies
81, Trinidad, West Indies
83, St. Vincent, West Indies
79, Barbados, West Indies
67, Grenadines, West Indies
85, Nile River, Egypt
125, Ghana, West Africa

Printed in the United States of America

Dedication

To my father, Earnest Dixon

To my muse, Brian Thomas

Acknowledgments

I thank God for His divine help. "You will call and the Lord will answer; you will cry for help, and He will say; here am I." Isaiah 58:9

I wish to thank Trinidad, West Indies for your people, experiences, peace and the beauty that nurtured my spirit while writing this book.

I want to thank Jessica Tilles of The Writer's Assistant. Your book and self-publishing coaching and professional knowledge made the realization of my dream a much easier journey.

Of course, my family and friends for their consistent encouragement and loving support, especially my niece, LaVonya Dixon-Jones, Priscilla Hunt, Norman Simmons, Pearl Smith and Ingrid Reynolds for your gracious comments. Thank you Niambi Brown-Davis for pushing, pushing and pushing me to not give up, and for accompanying and encouraging me to participate in several poetry readings. Jodi Yeldell, girl you so funny. Thank you for your friendship and sense of humor, "Wait, let me write that down." Calvin Rudy Jackson, my fantasy, thank you for your consistency, for keeping it real and always letting me be me.

To Cynthia Roby, my first real editor, I thank you for our insightful conversations and your honest critique. Delores Simmons, I thank you for your spiritual reflection and guidance. To Ella Curry, thank you for introducing me to Jessica and for your time explaining the do's and don't of the publishing process. To Trice Hickman, thank you for introducing me as a new author. To Pearl Smith, E. Ethelbert Miller, Lonise Bias, Jodi Yeldell and Niambi, I appreciate your friendship and reflective endorsements. To Pearl Cleage, thank you for being the inspiration for the title of my first book.

"What would you attempt to do if you knew you could not fail?"
~ Author Unknown

"Without loss and a great deal of pain one can never truly be inspired." —Zane

Dear Alma

Enjoy your journey —

Once you know . . .

Peace & Love

Earnell

9/12/10

Table of Contents

Change–It Can Only Get Better

Introduction

The essays and inspired poetry found on the pages of this book are meant for anyone who endeavors to take a journey inside themselves in search for self-awareness, love, beauty of nature, peace, or simply something to think about. These essays and poems were composed over time from my life journey and passion for travel. They come from the heart. Some created within minutes, others developed after years of travel, relationships, insight, pain, love, happiness, and praise. Each poem and essay is an experience—each having its own story—each prompted me to put pen to paper.

I hope you will enjoy this journey. It is my desire that by savoring the adventures and wisdom in this book, you will seek opportunities to explore the globe, enhance your life and become a gift to others.

I thank God for His divine help in writing this book. "You will call and the Lord will answer; you will cry for help, and He will say; here am I." Isaiah 58:9.

An open mind enhances the journey!

Live Hard So You Can Rest

Life Has Taught Me

Life has taught me
> That you can have more than one love of your life
> To let your man be "the man"
> Not to let others waste your moments
> Not to listen to disruptive music.

Life has taught me
> That laughter cures the ills of the soul
> It's easier to forgive after you forget
> Not to forgive is bondage
> That it's easy when God's in it.

Life has taught me
> Perfection can cause you to miss out on what you already have
> Shortcuts result in more obstacles and delays
> You don't have to fight every battle
> > the enemies will destroy themselves
> Don't try to please everybody; you will never get it right.

Life has taught me
> There is a difference between being happy and
> > wearing a façade of happiness
> Jealously is a liability
> > it generates no return on your investment
> Grief is personal
> > it lasts only as long as you need it
> Joy and sorrow are partners
> > you can't have one without the other.

Life has taught me
> To listen
> To enjoy your "Joy"
> To establish a relationship with God
> He will never abandon you.

Life has taught me
   Joy is found in giving
   Life is found in the taking
   Peace is found in being
   still
   content
   true and
   anxious for nothing.

Life has taught me to
   Trust God for all things.

I Decided

I decided
> To be happy most of the time
> To be free all the time
> To do what I want
>> when I want
>> where I want
>> how I want
>> as long as I want
>> without feeling
>> guilty, fearful or ashamed.

I decided
> To say "no" more often to protect my sanity and
> To say "yes" if it brings peace
> To listen with my heart and not my judgment
> To see with my spirit and not my sight
> To talk with a conscious and not my tongue.

I decided
> To always expect the best or accept less if there's no stress
> To be angry, sad, disappointed, and frustrated, sometimes
> It's my reality
> To smile frequently, it's my healthy
> To cry more often, it's my soul revival.

I decided
> To learn what I can and share it freely
> To enjoy each day
> Live in the present
> Cherish the past
> Expect the goodness of the future
> To love more, be discouraged less.

I decided to be content.
> It's peaceful.

Live Hard!

Live hard
  Love hard
    Work hard
      Care hard
        Sleep hard
          Play hard
            Pray hard
              Apologize hard
                Grieve hard
                  Cry hard.

Yes! Live hard with all the passion you can stand
When you die
You will need the "Rest."

Life Ain't No Joke!

Tangible, nonrefundable, no instant replays
It comes at you from every direction
Ready or not—full speed ahead
Brings joy if you want it
Sorrow when you don't.

Yes, life comes only once—full speed ahead
No recess, lunch break, napping or yours alone
Excitement, adventure, pain and pleasure.

No!
Life ain't no joke
It's tangible, nonrefundable, no instant replays
> Live it
>> Share it
>>> Feel it
>> Love it
>>> Want it
>>>> Take it!

Life ain't no joke,
But you can laugh yourself to death if you do it right!

Peace

Solitude

Flexible

Going with the flow

Rest uninterrupted

Appreciation

Don't go to peace, take it with you

When you have peace, you are comfortable with self

Can you be at peace when you are unhappy?

Truth…

Bliss

The hallway to bliss has many doors
Disappointment and success
Despair and optimism
Loneliness and friendship
Pain and tenderness
Poverty and prosperity
Transgression and worship
Self or God
Stay focused
Choose wisely.

Float

Trust God.
Take your foot off the peddle
Give Him the oars to your boat
Lay on your back
Eyes wide open
Sun on your face
Enjoy the ride.

Trust God.
He can dodge the rocks and
Satisfy your every need
Exceedingly and abundantly more
Than you can ask or think
According to your faith.

Trust God.
Be anxious about nothing
Relax
Ride the waves
Smell the salt in the sea.

Life is like water
It flows
Go with it …

Float!

September Sunsets
Life's senior years
The most glorious moments
As the sun descends into its glory
Adorned in its robe of many colors
Now is the time of your splendor
Anticipate—Know—Appreciate—Enjoy.

September Sunsets
Orange glows of achieved wisdom and knowledge
Blues for all life's pain, sorrow and regrets
Yellow yet you are optimistic because
It can only get better
Red moments of passion, love,
Parenthood and the joy of learning
You are royal purple children of God.

September Sunsets
After the sun of life has descended into
The horizon and
Your green light of youth is gone
The spirit is stronger and more peaceful
Your brilliance shines on
More radiant with opportunities to
Grow—to give—to love—
To dance to the quiet music of life.

September Sunsets
Full of colorful oil paintings across the heavens
Rainbow tinted clouds full of stories to tell
A lesson to share
A love that was given
Someone to care.
You are radiant September Sunsets.

Joy

Joy is watching my garden grow

Joy is good dance music

Joy is dancing

Joy is a soft juicy lingering consuming kiss

Joy is a good hair day

Joy is being surrounded by new books not knowing which one I
    want to read next

Joy is a hot outdoor shower

Joy is laying in my bed on my 100% Egyptian
    cotton 650-thread sheets

Joy is reading a book

Joy is flying to some where I've never been

Joy is good conversation with someone I don't know

Joy is eating Maryland blue crabs on a hot summer day

Joy is sleeping on the beach with nowhere else to be

Joy is being with my two sons in the same room at the same time

Joy is creating

Joy is receiving an unexpected package when away from home

Joy is watching a humming bird in flight

Joy is sitting on my North Carolina front porch
    watching cars pass on the country road

Joy is watching a brilliant sunset sitting on a cliff
    overlooking the sea

Joy is finishing a good book

Joy is kissing my 96-year-old mother and she knows who I am

Joy is buying a gift for anyone

Joy is riding through snow white Rock Creek Park
    in the early morning

Joy is knowing my children are happy

Joy is worshipping God.

In the Moment

Embrace the moment you are in
No plans, no agenda, no list
Appreciate your current state of peace.

New love is knocking at your door
You said you wanted more
Don't doubt the future or
Ponder the past
No matter how hard you try
Good things never last.

New opportunities, people, places and things
Cherish this precious moment you are in
Make wild passionate love whenever
Wherever
How often you can.

See your prayers answered and
Your hopes fulfilled
Laugh, sing, dance, relax
Breathe
Take hold
Be
Open
To the moment you are in.

Instant replay is not an option.

Love It or Lose It

29 Days

Then she met Michael
A kind and gentle soul.

Day one—he made her laugh.

Day three—she invited him into her world.

He was like a Kool cigarette
She had enjoyed so much
Inhaling him made her feel good inside
Helped release the tension
Her food taste better
Gave her something to do with her hands.

Day seventeen—she trusted him too soon.

She knew he was bad for her health
When he said prayer couldn't help
But, she did it anyway
He left a bitter taste in her mouth
She had to quit before she became ill
Withdrawal was painful at first, but doable
Quit smoking 20 years ago.

Day 29—he promised to never speak to her again.

Why does she miss what caused her pain?

You had your hurt.

Now, I've had mine!

The Package

Greek Islands, Rome, Venice, Naples, Florence and Capri
Irresistible
Men
Packaged
Sexy, alluring, handsome
Eyes of grey, green, hazel, caramel
Covered with long fluttering lashes
Olive complexions
Noses straight, large, small, crooked and hooked
Tall, short, slim, small-framed, sizable
Confident, jovial
Manly, sensual and sure
Long, straight, curly, black, sandy, blond, brown hair
Makes you want to melt
Like a bowl of chocolate ice cream
Exposed to the steaming hot summer sun.

Reserved smile on my face
Get me out of this place
Don't want to get caught with these thoughts
In Greece, "can we take your picture?"
They were compelling
Chiseled handsomeness
Umph, umph, umph
There should have been a patent on those Packages!

Wait, Mr. Postman
There's another Package
In my seat on a 747 at
New York's JFK
Waiting to return home to the West Indies

What do I see
Tall and black as Ebony trees
Thick steady and strong
BEAUTIFUL "Black" brothers are boarding the plane
Lord, have mercy
I forgot
Skin black as coal
Brown paper bags
Yellow as the sun
Oh, these brothers look like some serious fun
Tall, short, thick and thin
Hair wavy like the ocean
Kinky as a forest
Bald.

Locks neatly gathered, tied and flowing down their strong backs
Mustaches, beards or clean-shaven
The brothers are smooth, cool, confident and secure!

Yes, Mr. Postman I have another package
And, please put some insurance on this one.

Complaining

What's wrong with you?

You're always complaining!

You're in an unsatisfying relationship
You're complaining!

You get out the relationship
You're complaining!

You're lonely and want to meet someone
Complaining!

Then, you meet someone and you're
Still complaining!

What's wrong with you?
What do you want?
Do you know?
Call the Doctor!

I Don't Know What I Am Doing

I met someone.

I met someone who fulfills my deepest fantasies.

I have someone
Who is my Reality.

I don't know what I am doing.

I think I need them both.

The Reality loves me
The Fantasy…

Every morning in the real world I wake up in my Fantasy.
Every night my Reality becomes my Fantasy.

I am confused.

I need the stability of my Reality yet I crave the Fantasy that
gives me
JOY—PEACE—BEAUTY—HOPE—HAPPINESS.

I don't know what I am doing.

Can a Fantasy become Reality?
Can Reality evolve into Fantasy?

I must know.

How would I know?

Is there something I can
do
be
say?

Can I have them both or none
So I can know what I am doing?

Time Out

Take a break—
Don't date
Clean your house
Read a book
Take a trip
Have a fling
Learn chess
Exercise
Volunteer
Call your parents
Have another fling
Regroup
Support a cause
Take a class
Date
Get a check-up
Pray
Honor yourself
Be friends
Love self, first.

Okay, now you're ready!

It's just me here
In this little house.

The rooms are small and
The furniture is sparse
But it's okay
There is love here.

Nothing fancy
Clean windows in every room
I can see out real good
Plenty natural light coming in.

I have a small fridge
But, it's always filled and content.

There's plenty of closet space
Never had a lot of baggage
Always tidy
Don't like no mess.

A little bed
Cozy and warm
Won't let me fall.

The outside is authentic and cute
Passersby always make flattering remarks, say
"We look real inviting."

Yes, it's just me here in this little house
Could sure use some company
But, please
Leave your shoes at the door.

You Missed the Point

You missed the point
I said what I meant
But you did not hear
The door to my heart was open
But you did not enter
This little house is clean and uncluttered
This little house is me.

Love, peace and forgiveness are free
Let go of your misery
So you can see.

This Little House #2

That man just crawled up under my skin
Made himself at home in this little house
I tried to shake him, but he fell in love with the skin I'm in.

My door was open
My heart unsecured
His kind voice filled my every room with his strength and peace
Then he smiled in my eyes
Took a bath in my fear
Hung his scent in my soul
And stored his goodness in the basement of my heart.

Said I made him want to be a better man
I could not argue
Because my everything was in order
And I do the best I can.

So, he made me his new address
His furniture fit
He's receiving his mail
And his *good* friends stop by all the time
Humor Me
Helpful Harry
Baby Love
You Make Me Feel Like a Natural Woman
Won't You Be My Number One and
Respect Yourself.

Food is never a problem
Bills get paid
On time

Yes, I sure do love this skin I'm in
And home never felt better.

By the way
He left his shoes outside to air
So I just brought them in
And put them in the closet
with the rest of our stuff!

Here We Go Again

Another dude?
Here we go again—what makes you think you love me?

Is it my self-confident,
know where I'm going,
like where I've been,
assertive self?

Is it my creamy hot chocolate fudge complexion or
my kiss that lingers long after I have left the room?

Here we go again—what makes you think you love me?

Because
My spirit arrives before you
    see my alluring face,
    smell my intoxicating scent,
    hear my velvet voice or
    feel my seductive touch?

Because
I shower you with compliments and praise, the way I look you in
    the eye when I ask for what I want or because I unselfishly
    give you what you need?

Because
I know there is a time and place for spontaneity, passion, fun,
    worship, work, attitude, patience, quiet discussion and
    forgiveness or is it because I can still hear the music of your
    hope long after everyone else has gone?

Because
I carry the dreams of my children on my shoulders until they can
   bear the weight alone or because I keep the door to my heart
   open to my parents when they can no longer live alone?

Here we go again—what makes you think you love me?

Is it the way I stroke your strong oppressed back trampled daily
   by every social economic criminal ideology with my tears,
   embrace your manhood and decisions without question,
   support your hopes and dreams, comfort your
   disappointments or our mutual love and respect for God?

Is it the way I listen when I don't want to, understand you when
   no one else can or my willingness to share and listen until it's
   all okay, with us?

Here we go again—what makes you think you love me?

Because
I live free or because
I respect your freedom?

Because
all I need from you cost nothing or
all I want is your respect and tenderness?

Here we go again—okay, I love you, too!

Agape

He did not take my love
    He received it
He did not require my love
    He accepted it
He did not abuse my love
    He enjoyed it
He did not lose my love
    He nurtured the agape in me.

Why Does It Hurt?

Why does this love lost hurt so bad?
Because I loved him most, just before he left.
We were so close.

The earth stood still whenever he assured me,
"Baby, I'll take care of it,"
and he always did.

We just fit!

He let me rub his feet and between his toes,
Trim his mustache,
hold his hand and
fix his plate,

And, whenever I asked myself, "What can I do for him?"
It was because of who he was and what he gave
Love and Joy to everyone.

Why does this love lost hurt so bad?

Because life doesn't always give you what you want
But he satisfied
My every need with
Kindness,
Attention,
Affection,
An ear to my soul.
We were so close...
Home every day.
Calls every day.
Love every day.

The sound of his key in the door...
    "Baby"

"You're so soft"
"You look nice"
"I miss you."

Why does this love lost hurt so bad?

Because I can't
 Touch him or
Rub him
I can't talk to him, or
dance with him,
hold or sleep with him.
No, I can't even Thank him.

We were so close.

We spoke just this morning
Laughed
"How do you feel"
"Everything will be all right"
"I Love you, Baby"
"Enjoy your day."

And then,
He died.

Somebody's Been Sleeping

She was accustomed to
the same someone
sleeping
in her bed
every night…

When

When I'm walking down the street
The sun is hot
I feel him on my skin.

When the wind blows
Suddenly
I feel his gentle fingers in my hair.

When the dove sings while watching me
I feel him in my spirit.

When the rain falls on my face
I feel his thick lips caress my mouth.

When our song plays on the radio
I feel the weight of his feet dancing on my toes.

When I look upon his picture
I feel the rumble of his joyous laughter in my soul.

When I cry
I feel his long, strong, dark arms
Contain me
I hear him
Pray for us.

Infomercial

"Mature" widow available for you
Before she loses her demurer!

Looking for love in all the right places
You need not apply if she can't see your faces.

Much to offer
The right guy and
Here's the reason why
Don't give stress—won't take your mess
Affectionate, tried and true
Emotionally, physically and spiritually well
Ain't bad to look at, too
Lust with the best, but trust is a must
Her love is ready for you
Looking for same
If interested, please submit your name.

A picture sir
So she can see
An address, income, health records (just kidding) and
Why you think you're the guy for her.

Married, gay, DL, incarcerated, broke, substance abusers,
        toothless couch potatoes
Need not apply
Ages 47 to 65, only
She's in her prime and that's no lie
Want a monogamous lasting relationship
Will give you all her love
An intimate long-term relationship
Until the Good Lord welcomes one of you above.

Hope you like this infomercial
I think it's really neat
Because you can believe me
It wasn't cheap!

Just Because

I Don't Feel Like It!

Sometimes, I just don't feel like it!
Going the extra mile or putting on that bogus smile.
Saying "yes" when I really mean "no,"
Going where I don't want to go.

I just don't feel like combing my hair,
When I know that's not where they stare;
Trying to be pretty when I'm gorgeous just the way I am,
Trying to be thin when I love this phat I'm in.

No! I don't feel like it!
Going somewhere to work, to church, to visit the sick
Caressing your dick!
Sleeping with one eye open
Waiting to hear your key in the door
I don't think I want to live like this no more.

My body don't want to get up at 5:30 a.m.
To work for somebody who don't appreciate I'm here.

My hands didn't want to prepare
A hot meal that no one ate or
Put on that brand new $400 dress
Only my girlfriends will appreciate.

My ears don't want to hear
Gangster rap!
You slam the door because we can't agree to disagree;
The cell phone ringing
    in the movies just when the plot thickens,
    in church when the Pastor is praying,
    in the car when I'm trying to concentrate
    on the baby in the back seat.

My eyes don't want to see
Her shake her half-dressed behind every time I turn on the TV.

No, I don't feel like it!
Oh well, maybe tomorrow
But, only if I feel like it.

A Breeze in My Pocket

Let me catch some of this breeze
Put it in my pocket
Take it home
It's hot there!

When I open the door
His desire greets me
With a heat so intense that
Only this breeze
in my pocket
will bring him close enough to touch
It's so hot here.

My lips are parched
A hot river flows
Down my legs
His touch
Burning
Ouch
Breeze
Where are you?

If I go into the kitchen
His flames are there.
Ouch!

Mr. Johnson has the bedroom
So hot
I have to take a drink
Or he won't leave.

We really need to
Release!
It's hot here.

Ahh...
This breeze is just what we needed.

Jodi

"Look, Girlfriend,
I'm 59 years old.
I don't need a long range plan.
I can wake in the morning,
Shout crap to the wind,
Do what I want to for the day!"

I Be

I don't stress
From you I don't expect any less
I don't worry
I be.

I don't envy
I don't fret
I don't complain
I don't want
I be.

I don't fuss, but
You can if you must
I don't feel ill unwanted unloved
Someone is watching my back from above
I lack nothing
I just be.

Yes Ma'am

Guess you mean well, but

Yes Ma'am to me!?

I'm sick of you folks calling me Yes Ma'am
My gray is covered
I can dance longer and harder than you
I still look good in my one-piece on the beach
I'm polished, I'm sharp, and I'm kept.

I'm not old, yet
You must see something I don't … how dare you!

My Story

It's my story.
You may have a part in it
A role only you can play
An epic wonder for all to see, but
The curtain rises and falls on me.

It's my story.
God wrote the screen play and designed the set
His music is awesome
The props are few
He lets me improvise and sing, too.

Grace is my understudy
Holds me up when
I am too weak to perform
If I change the script and
Make the right choice
It's a blessing, but
My dreams are left on the thrashing floor
When I don't learn my lessons.

His sets can be elaborate
With a cast of many
The script discerning and
My lines can be funny
Wisdom is often my understudy and
Grace helps with my lines
I forget often times.

Surprise endings add mystery and
The plots are timeless
But, that's okay
Because
God is my Executive Producer and
It's my story.

Satisfied

I know who I am and I'm satisfied
Did not just arrive, but
Traveled many roads and seas
Flew where I needed to be
Saw what I needed to see.
I'm satisfied.

Fresh opportunities
To learn and share
To error and repent
To understand and grow
To wish and trust
To seek balance.
I'm satisfied.

Had I not been inquisitive, open and free
The people, places, experiences
Would not have shaped me.
I'm satisfied.

God's love and
Your affection made me
Have a dream
To be all that I can be.
I'm satisfied.

Though still under construction
I am under budget and on schedule.

I am satisfied.

Ricardo

When he flew into my life he did not know he would never leave
Trinidad.

He did not look like the others
He was glamorous and free
Feathers vibrant like garden orchids
Magenta orange and green
in Trinidad.

His song an early morning alarm
Music for our guests
Filled each room
in Trinidad.

Early to bed
Early to rise
Singing loudly with his friends
Two brown doves
Peered into the kitchen when I was not looking every day
in Trinidad.

Curious and confident was he
Often my only company
He heard every word
Saw every scene
Kept my secrets
in Trinidad.

Ricardo, Ricardo, you okay?
No sight—no sound
Where can you be
I miss your company after
You left me
in Trinidad.

My Caribbean is Leaving Me

My Caribbean is leaving me.

Instead of Reggae, it's jazz;
Where Calypso and Soca should be,
R&B has become the song for me.
And though the music is still lives in my bones,
I now choose to dance alone.

What happened to my love for callaloo, plantains,
    breadfruit and jerk?
It's now broccoli, green beans, baked potatoes, soup.

Oh, the natural splendor of the mountains, sky, and sea;
Each island is beginning to look the same to me.

The love that was present now lives in my heart
Believing it can only get better,
I must open self to a brand new start.

Oh, Caribbean
Oh, West Indies
My People
My culture
My being
I Love You so.

If I leave thee
Please, never leave me.

*This poem was written as I anticipated leaving the
West Indies after living there for five enchanted years.*

Come Before His Presence

God's Wardrobe

Joseph wore a coat of many colors,
our Father, in heaven, has a closet of many coats.

The universe is His closet. In the late evening He wears midnight-blue skies to cover His head. When He wants to show off, the shining stars are worn for bling. He wears the untouched snow as His slippers, quiet and soft as He walks among the giant pine trees sweeping them with the hem of His winter white-garment.

He uses the stillness of the early morning dew laden with fragrance of roses, jasmine, and eucalyptus to awaken the sunrise, and then He fans the freshness of a spring rain to create 3-D Technicolor rainbows that sparkle over the Caribbean Sea. When He wants to rustle the waters, He whispers to splash the waves upon the seashore where soft white sand and a million seashells adorn His fingers.

The imposing snowcapped Alps of Italy, the overwhelming Alaskan mountains, and the solitude of Mt. Fuji flaunt the majesty of His power and awesomeness.

God wears His coat layered in red roses, purple orchids, white azaleas, blue tulips and yellow sunflowers when His court of toucans, parrots, eagles, and cardinals await His presence in lovely song.

Yes, the universe is His closet of many coats!

He wears the sea as deep as the tallest mountains around His waist and the clouds as His crown, never the same spectacle twice. The sun, moon, Jupiter, and Mars are the feathers in His cap. Rubies, amber, silver, sapphires, and emeralds He has in abundance to show off His creativity. He wears His patchwork pastures, grazing hills, quiet valleys, rolling brooks, and cool streams to sometimes accessorize. He covers His shoulders with the wind; uses the lighting to see in the dark and thunder to announce His coming.

God's universe is His closet of many coats, but His most valued possession is His precious love for us. He wears it in a diamond locket around His neck for every living thing to see.

Jackie's in Negril

As I approached the cliff's edge a hush engulfed me like a heavy invisible fog. I sensed God's presence. No soaring birds just the command of the ocean. My spirit said, "Yes, Lord," my body stood still as my soul waited for a word from Him. Afraid to move not wanting to lose the peace, I knew my God was at Jackie's on the reef.

Hear God's ocean lullaby
Self Awareness is there.

Sense His movement in the trade winds
God touches your soul
Moving through your spirit
Liberation is there.

Feel His warm humid breath
A blanket of dew finding rest upon your skin
Just enough to let you know
Peace and comfort are there.

A reef in Negril called Jackie's
If you are still and open you can speak, tell Him all
He is never too busy to give you His undivided attention
Nothing and no one is more important than you
Faith and hope abides there.

Experience God at Jackie's.

Quiet

Quiet piercing when unexpected
Always welcomed
Less abrupt in the darkness of night.

No TV no radio no MP3 no cell phone
No meetings, no thinking, no rush to everywhere
No arguments, no shouting
No children, no parents, no other calling your name
Quiet.

Quiet place
Quiet prayer
Quiet tears
Listen
Be still, be aware.

Hear breath
Hear loveliness
Hear wind move over you
Hear ocean that never stops
Hear the raindrops
Hear dewdrops
Hear snowflakes drift midair
Hear birds sing
Hear your tears fall
Hear everything
Hear nothing at all.

Quiet is piercing when unexpected
Always welcomed
Less abrupt in the darkness of night.
Be quiet be still

Hear self
Hear your body relax~rest~rejuvenate
Hear peace
Hear God
Hear the answer you have been waiting for.

Rain Combo

Rain!

Here she comes! Can't you hear her? And, she's bringing along her friends, Cool Breeze and Lovely Scent.

Sometimes they bring a disruption to your day, but if you stop and listen, you'll know she brings peace, calm, music, and nourishment.

Rain!

Look at them. Rain refreshes and makes lovely music as she touches everything along her way.

Listen! She never comes alone; Cool Breeze watches her back quietly as its soothing presence blows the earth with freshness.

And after every natural and beautiful thing has been washed and blown dry, Lovely Scent brings up the rear leaving a clean fragrance that lingers if you pay attention and welcome her aroma.

Rain!

She never travels alone.
She's the leader of the most majestic combo,
    Look
        Listen
                Experience them

Their performance is free!

You can't schedule their appearance
So be ever so ready to enjoy them the next time they're in
your area.

This poem was written as I sat on my veranda in Trinidad. In the quiet dawn of early morning it suddenly began to rain. Unwilling to go inside, I gathered my book, cup of tea and sat captivated by the scent, the sound and tranquility of the falling rain.

The Piano

What would it require to master the piano?
Not only play
I want to sound like an angel
Playing the piano.

The echo of the keys
The comfort and rhythm of the music
Must sound like the fingertips of angels gently stroking each key.

When I play
The listener must think of the clear blue sky
In the midst of the day
That deepest blue
Distant and unending
But looks so close you could touch it.

An angel playing the piano
Resonating calm security and consolation
A delicate penetrating tune
You can see travel
Through the tree tops
In the early morning
After the sun has risen and there is
No sound except the dew falling and
The leaves dancing in the breeze.

Yes,
I would love to play the piano
My fingers must let my heart and soul express itself
So you only see
An angel sending sounds from heaven.

Yes, I want to play the piano.

So High

Looking at the distant mountaintops
Carpeted in hues of green
I want to walk on that lush carpet covering those mountains.

I'm so high the birds are flying beneath my feet
I can feel the trees between my toes.

Large cotton clouds close enough to touch
Moving north in the cool summer breeze against my face
Makes me want to cuddle in the arms of God
Comforted in His peaceful place.

Do you think this is where the ancestors rest
Riding in the clouds touching our spirits
Protecting and guiding us
Providing every good and perfect gift?

Oh, I'm walking upon the mountaintops
I shall touch those clouds and learn from them
I will return soon, but for now
My desire is to watch
The birds soar beneath my feet
Feel the trees between my toes.

Trees

Always looking reaching up
Dressed in their robes of forest green
Singing praises
Solo or as members of the Wilderness Choir
Sun, rain, snow, hail, wind, day or night
Trees

In
Perpetual
Unending
Everlasting
Continuous Praise
Trees

In
Permanent
Uninterrupted
Eternal
Constant Praise
Trees

Grounded deep in what matters
Surrounded by love
Givers of life
Steadfast unmovable
Bending with the breeze
Trees

In
Lasting
Unbroken Praise
Trees

As diverse as we
Resourceful Palms
Black Ebony
Solid Oak
Giant Redwood
Resilient Teak
Surviving Odum
Ancient Cypress
Weeping Willow
Colorful Dogwood
Sweet Magnolia
Trees

They look to the Lord from whence cometh their strength.
Do they know something we don't?

River Nile

A serene resourceful place of beauty and antiquity.
Out of God's heart flows rivers of living water,
and one is called the
River Nile.

Orange and purple horizon rises on the east
enchanting sunsets close the day in the west.
Like a wide sparkling stream, she flows
through Egypt's center.
People washing their clothes, cars and
horses; bathing in the
River Nile.

Resource for
clay bricks
transportation
irrigation
the
River Nile.

People
gathering
swimming
eating
sleeping by the
River Nile.

In front of the ship, hundreds of seagulls,
ducks, geese, and cranes settle on the
tranquil waters, relaxing with us. Quietly
they scatter that we may sail.

After passing, they elegantly resettle to resume
their restful place.

Do not be deceived; every good and perfect
gift is from above
And, so it is the
River Nile.

Sailing down the River Nile, Egypt.

2000 Years Before

Soft chimes ringing from the deck
large picture windows encircle
the dining room filled with guests
quietly chatting as the steam boat
moves effortlessly from the dock
to sail up the Nile River.

The scene slowly transcends
from the frantic Cairo city limits
to a quiet rural place
the shores come into view
as you imagined them to be 2000 years
before serene framed by palms, tall
stalks of sugar cane trees bursting with
figs and coconuts golden wheat swaying
in the quiet breeze.

Beyond the fertile green shores
stand tall majestic desert mountains
covered in dusty hues of red, orange and brown.

Same as imagined 2000 years before
Nubian villages of red clay dwellings
children playing
invisible women covered from head to toe in flowing black
men walking, working and smoking in long white robes
barking dogs running
belabored donkeys hauling the harvest
unflappable oxen plowing the soil.

On the peaceful Nile River same as 2000 years before
your skin is awakened by just enough gentle wind
to let you know this is real watching the men sail
Feluccas, fish and relax under the spectacular
purple horizon the sky dry and faultless.

Suddenly a hush settles over the dining room
no one is speaking we all have the same experience
overwhelmed by the magic of the moment
as we feel 2000 years of history.

Time stands still envisioning Abraham, the
disciples and Paul walking on the same shores
doing the same things.

Quiet and unnoticed, I left the dining room and cried.

Absorbing the majesty and tranquility of the
Mediterranean Sea, Jeff Majors' soothing Sacred CD
is playing in the background. The peacock blue sky is
clear. It is a beautiful and bright sunny day. Not a cloud
for miles to distract from the enormity of the turquoise
sea surrounding me. Vibrant from the reflection of the
sun is a perpetual sea of white diamonds.

God sprinkled these diamonds
Thankful that I can see
His magic stardust
Sprinkled upon the sea
Few appear—blink and there are many diamonds
there for me
Perspective—is what you choose to see.

Glittering reflections appear as
Crystals
Diamonds upon the sea.

Lord, Thank You for my sight!

God Is

Love

The smallest ripple in the pond
The power in a crushing tidal wave
The speed of the hummingbird's wings
The confidence of the soaring eagle
The still peace of evening twilight
The early morning sunrise of a new day
A cloudless sky

God is
Birth
Fulfilling life
Peaceful death
Grandma's hands
Obedient child

God is the source of joy
Wisdom, faith, and grace
Ability
Giving and forgiveness

God is
A favorite song
A peaceful slumber
A long awaited telephone call
A hug
A lingering kiss

Gratitude for what is pure, what is just, what is true
Answered and unanswered prayers
You and me
Our destiny

God is...

Family and Friends

Sister

Sometimes she laughs
but I'm not satisfied
it's true enough.

She loves everyone
but I'm not sure
they love her back.

She is beautiful and sincere
will give you
what she doesn't have
if you ask.

When she's here
she brings the thunder, lightning, and rain
of a much needed summer storm.

When she's not
the heart is full of
heavy smoke.

She cries.
She dreams a thousand dreams.
She's somebody's friend.
I wish she were mine.

Dedicated to my sister, Bernett Dixon, 1957- 2005.

Unhappy Father

Standing at Heaven's pearly gates
Where the righteous enter
awaits the unhappy father of the bride.

"Husband," he said, "Your love was
great for my daughter,
but now
her heart is broken
because
you left too soon...
she hasn't finished dancing!"

Kids

You got kids?
>Do you love them?
>Show them?
>Hug them?

Do you teach them?
>Who God is?
>How to love themselves and care for others?
>To always look out for their Mother, Father,
>Sister, Brother?

Do you tell them?
>How beautiful they are?
>How proud you are?
>They're your shining star?

You got kids?
>Love them
>Then
>Let them go!

We do the best we can with what we got.
If it wasn't enough, sorry.
If it was too much, we tried too hard.
If it was just right, "you're welcome!"

Grandma's Favorite Recipe

Grandma, how you make life taste so good?
You so kind and strong and flavorsome
Always filling
Keeps us coming back for more.

Well child, I got myself a secret recipe
Been in this family for generations.

First, wash out all the pots, countertops, and utensils
Of jealousy, gossip, greed, and hate
They can spoil the best of ingredients.

Take hope out the fridge several hours in advance
It must be used at room temperature
To rise above all doubt.

I use the Give of Myself spoon to mix.
Stir in some adventure, curiosity and optimism
You want the flavor to be exciting
Slowly pour wisdom, faith and some patience
Into the soul
It guarantees a good consistency.

Marinade the spirit
In forgiveness, love and peace for strength
While you add equal parts of laughter, hugs and kisses
They sweeten the taste
Simmer in prayer overnight to ensure everything settles in your
spirit.

Finally, climb three flights of stairs to maintain physical stamina
Garnish yourself fashionably and always decent
Stylish and elegant
A good presentation encourages the appetite.

Grandma's secret recipe is best served at room temperature with plenty of Thanksgiving.

Preparation time: 24 / 7
Servings: Enough for everyone

Bon Appétit!

Family and Friends

Many are my family friends
Like the gentle waves that support a ship
Each having a purpose for our relationship.

Gentle as a ripple in the pond
Responsive with calming encouragement
Correcting and comforting me
Through times of floods and famines.

You surround me like a nourishing vine
Oxygen that breathes life and support
Company encouraging happiness
Giving spiritual guidance for good decisions.

Like a flawless summer cloud
Giving shade when life is too hot
Backs as strong as a Cyprus tree
Planted in African soil
Constant, encouraging, loving and true
My family and friends are gifts from God
Beautifully wrapped to
Pray
Give
Receive
Laugh
Cry
Dance
Play
And help Me.
No wonder I look to the heavens from whence cometh my
strength
And the nourishment of my family and friends.

I appreciate You.

Nubian Sister

Her hate is fueled by pain
empathy feeds her despair.

Skin Black as the deepest cave
where her culture, family and self knowledge
was buried never to be found
on the journey to Cape Coast and
the dungeons of Elmira Castle.

Eloquence radiates
in her voice and in the movement of her limbs
as she strolls through every welcomed and forbidden place.

Her loins still primed to birth the kings and queens of the world
once raped, tortured, disrespected, and discarded
yet, she's the Mother of the Church
the endearing trainer
therapist, lover, sister, and steadfast friend.

Her tenderness wants to forget, forgive, and love her captors
because they have skeletons that live in shadows stealing
their joy.

She travels home
renews her spirit
reconnects with her ancestors
recovers her real meaning and
presents self to her
Nubian Brothers.

Closer Than A Brother in a Foreign Land

From your Mothers, sisters, daughters, lovers and friends
Brothers in every foreign land
You are our source—without you we do not exist
You are the moisture in our tears
The heat in our passion
The grace in our hope
The wisdom in our understanding and
The love of our lives.

We see you brothers in America, Africa, Asia, South America,
    the Caribbean, Europe, and the Middle East
Selling peanuts, fake designer bags, and t-shirts
Drugging and drinking, disrespecting and abusing
Loitering, begging, stealing, killing and running
On city streets corners, in back alleys, big cities and small towns
On TV and radio, in gangster videos and movies
On the planes, trains, buses, boats, and subways
In blue collar and no collar
Wearing too few suits in too many courtrooms, jails, hospitals, and
    the morgues.

We need brothers in every foreign land to keep it together,
    because
You're often wrongfully used, accused, and abused
Denied your brilliance, passion, and pain,
Stealing your manhood and claiming you're insane.
Brothers in all foreign lands
You are our fathers, brothers, sons, lovers and friends
You are the help we did not know we needed
The relief from our pain
The source of our hope
The foundation under my feet and
The muse of our story.

We know there are brothers in America, Africa, Asia, South
    America, the Caribbean, Europe, and the Middle East
Teaching, preaching and giving
Caring fathers, husbands, and sons doing the best you can
You love, protect, fear, laugh, want, work, cry,
You bleed, you die just like everybody else, you try.

We are proud of you brothers in every foreign land
Writing literature, directing movies and making music,
Winning gold medals and championships,
Owning corporations, selling real estate, negotiating deals,
Going to the moon, defending your country,
Making history and breaking barriers.

Brothers in every foreign land

We love you—we want you—we need you
Without you we are like
A ship out of water, we cannot float
A tree without roots, we cannot grow
A bird with no wings, we cannot fly
A brain without a mind, we cannot think
A body without a soul, we cannot love.

Brothers—when you believe in us we succeed.

Death

Death
Anger
Pain
Sorrow
Sadness
Despair
Sudden
Overwhelming
Guilt
Denial
Interruption
Irritation
Lost
Love
Forever
Gone
Alone
Loneliness
Forgiveness
Relief
Reminisce
Remember
Reflect
Rebirth

Change–It Can Only Get Better

Black Caucus

What do we need you for?

Our men are still being locked up
Just for being who they are
Strange fruit has become
Bananas boxed in crates and left to rot while
Our women and children are
Starving for nourishment, protection, and love.

Black Caucus—what do you do, do, do?
Who are you?
Why do I have to ask?
What do you stand for?

What Katrina did not take, you "gave" to them
Our homes
Our land
Our blood, sweat, and tears
You not watching our backs
Standing up for our little piece of Martin's dream
"That one day..."

Black Caucus
Mercy, mercy me
What's goin' on, elected officials?
Can't you see you Black just like me?

My daughter has HIV and can't afford to get healthy
My son is still on crack
Who is in the courts watching our backs?
My man don't have no job, but
He got a Ph.D in philosophy from the University
That affirmative action did not fund.

Black Caucus
Is one Oprah bigger than the fifty states?

There's a saying, if you don't stand for somethin' you'll fall
    for anything ...
The big house
Deceptive all expense paid trips
Invisible power, watered down shaken and thrown out
Fancy cars
Publicity
Octobers in DC
Partee.

We need you to stand for your people
Protect our
Homes
Children
Education
Health
Economics
Our FREEDOM.

Black Caucus
Black like me?
Let me see!

Crossing the Atlantic

Dear Journal... *"To travel is to experience history."*

Bottomless Atlantic Ocean as far as the eye can see,
To my surprise its as beautiful as the Caribbean Sea.

December 8

Each day, connecting with the ancestors
That endured this same Middle Passage
Crammed into the black bottomless pit of the slave ships
100 million
Stolen
Sold
Abandoned into slavery.

Believe their pain.

They survived captivity
One month
Two months
Three months in castle dungeons
Awaiting the horrific journey to an unknown place and time.

Imagine their anxiety.

Pushed into the pits of hell through the
Door of No Return
Torture, sickness, broken bones, murder, and suicide
Swallowed by the intimidating sea
I want to feel the
agony
unknown

fear
misery
suffering
loneliness
despair.

Experience their hopelessness.

December 10

Clear sunlit sky
Hovering over the ocean
A heavy gray storm cloud is in the distance
Thick mist appears from its center
God is gathering His souls from the ocean
Up to heaven.

Redeemed.

December 13

No weapon formed against me shall prosper.

I am in the ship's luxury spa having the works—seaweed wrap,
massage, facial, manicure and pedicure—and the Eastern
European technicians are serving ME!

I am here.
I am capable.
I am resourceful.
I am productive.
I am independent.

I am a survivor.
I am loved.
I am free.

"He lifted me out of the slimy pit, out of the mud and mire;
He set my feet on a rock and gave me a firm place to stand."
— Psalm 40:2

Fix Your Face!

Sister Girlfriend Woman
fix your face.

You step onto the elevator with no sparkle or joy.
I see you walking, sledging down the street
distracted, despondent, full of despair.

Why do you look so sad?
What happened to you?
With you?
Girlfriend, you look mean.
You got Attitude!

I see you in
a DC office
on a New York train
walking the streets of Rome
leaving your home
on the beach
in the air to everywhere, I see you there.

With plenty attitude, attitude, attitude!

There's mean in your eyes,
no glide in your stride.
Got something good to say?
No way!

Sister this is universal, you're the
short and tall
rich and poor
dark and light

lean and phat
young, beautiful women.

Why do you look so mean first thing
        in the morning
                noontime
                        or night?
                                Are your panties too tight?

Where is "Good Morning"
"Hello"
"Enjoy your day"
You have "Anything" positive to say?

What's the problem, Girlfriend?
Get over it!
Take back your joy.
Life is knocking at your door.
You have EVERYTHING to be thankful for.

Everybody doesn't have
a comforting Mother a phone call away,
a son who is doing the best he can
a husband who adores her and is willing to support her every
dream!
Be Thankful!

You have beautiful, healthy children.
You have a j-o-b!
Be Happy!

You can see the sunset change its colors every evening,
the moon when it is full and bright,
all the colors of the rainbow,
what a spectacular sight.
You can hear the birds sing their symphony,
music that can make you dance all your cares away.
Make that gloom and doom leave you anyway.
Be Grateful!

You can feel your lover's whisper, smell his favorite cologne and taste
his love!
Sister, take it light.

In the scheme of things
When you flip the switch, the lights come on.
When you turn the handle, the toilet flushes.
You bathed and clothed yourself this morning and
your feet took you where you wanted to go!

So, the next time I see you, replace that attitude with
        a pep in your step,
                a smile in your heart, and
                        grace on your face.

For this is the day the Lord made, Rejoice and Be Glad in It!

Umm, Something to Think About...

Who were you yesterday?
Who are you today?

Are you the best you can be?
Do you know what the best is?

Do you think you need to change?
Why?
How?

Is God still in charge?
If not, why not?

Do you love God today as much as you did yesterday?
More?
Less?
How do you know?

Umm, something to think about ...

Dark Dungeon

Dark dungeon
Is a neighborhood in life
Easy to enter
Difficult to depart.

Despair loneliness disappointment and grief
Usher you in
Depression at the door
Holds the key
Rooms painted black brown and blue
No windows
No love laughter or joy
No music—limited food
Few resting places
Sadness and sorrow share your bed
Hopelessness feeds your pain.

There are many directions to the Dark Dungeon
You can travel
Troubled Children Lane
Ailing Parents Avenue
Unemployed Circle
Broken Heart Boulevard
Death's Parkway
Unpaid Bills Street
Incarcerated Court or
Hopeless Freeway.

Warning!
Keep out of the Dark Dungeon
Don't lie down—stay alert
Take the righteous road
Keep grace in front and don't slip
Some places are easy to enter, but difficult to depart.

Troubles

Hey!
Troubles don't live here no more,
They had to go!
They were making my skin so sore.

They stank up the place
Left baggage in my heart;
Worry on my mind, and
Abused my joy.

I kicked them out last night.
This morning I
Bathed in some Praise,
Soaked in some Faith,
Then rested in Hope.

Hey, what's that I hear ...
Troubles knocking at my door?

Didn't I tell you?

Can't come back here no more!
Space is gone for you and your kind.
My friend Grace is here and we're filling my spirit with some
Wisdom
Love
Peace and Joy.

So, there is no room for you through this door!
Troubles, I hate to burst your bubble, but you don't live here
    no more!

Once You Know

Once you know your full brilliance and intellect
    You're obligated

Once you know your full potential and availability
    You're obligated

Once you know your true kindness and generosity
    You're obligated

Once you exploit your talent
    You're obligated

Once you know your history and worth
    You're obligated

Once you know
    You're obligated to make a difference

Once you know...
    What are you going to achieve?

No More Excuses

You did not have the rent
Because your designer party shoes
Were more important.

You failed the exam
Because you did not study.

You were late for work
Because you did not leave on time.

You were abused, neglected, and scorned
Because you tolerated it.

Your children did not learn swearing from their friends
They heard it at home.

You're not fat because of thyroids
You eat too much.

You're not a homeowner because your income is too low
Your expensive car was your priority.

He stopped calling
Not because he's working overtime
He's cheating!

She's not sleeping with you
Because she just wants to be your friend
She just doesn't like you!

No more excuses—do better.

Economics

There is no world peace because
It's not economically profitable...

It's not too difficult for the feds and industry to get it right
It's not economically profitable...

Incurable diseases continue to plague the world population
    because
It's economically profitable...

Education is not equal because of learning difficulties
It's economically profitable...

World political, social, academic and financial poverty are not
    impossible to eradicate
They exists because it's economically profitable...

To the rich powerful few.

Obama's Prayer

We pray for President Barack H. Obama knowing that

GOD IS THE SPINE IN HIS BACK.

We pray that God will always bless him with

the WISDOM of Solomon,

the FAITH of Abraham, and

the COURAGE of David.

We pray that God will PROTECT him

as He protected Daniel in the lion's den.

Blood Diluted and Watered Down

Ghana was the home or gateway from which most West Africans endured the Middle Passage, to the so-called "New World"—North America, South America and the Caribbean, i.e., the black Diaspora. Throughout my short, but up close and personal journey, it became clear that we came from a strong "sense of community with a foundation of integrity and pride," which the Ghanaians have maintained. However, because of over 350 years of prejudice, oppression, and perpetuated self-hatred, we have become diluted. Some have become physically, morally and economically watered-down, thinned out.

We no longer resemble our ancestors, but instead come in new colors of chocolate brown, sunrise yellow and caramel cream; brown, green, gray, hazel eyes; keen noses, big ears, thin lipped; long, wavy, shinny hair. Diluted. It's not our fault, but results from centuries of pre-calculated eradication.

The moral values of our ancestors have digressed, for example stealing from one another was not tolerated in one small village I visited. Driving through southern Ghana, we passed a man lying dead on the street who had been stoned to death by the local citizens because he was caught stealing! I did not see liquor stores or rum shops on every other corner. Only a very few drink and I don't remember seeing anyone smoking a cigarette. I was told that drinking and smoking are frown upon because of strong religious beliefs and it is not considered a healthy pastime. Ghana has the highest percentage of Christians, 60% in West Africa, but the belief in traditional animist religions is still extremely common. Blasphemy and swearing of any sort is unacceptable. Did you know in Trinidad you can be jailed for swearing in public?

Our ancestors practiced shared economics. People worked together. The small children gave their earnings to the older siblings, which contributed up the hierarchy, to help and support each other. If one vendor did not have the article you wanted to buy they found a colleague who sold it, so you could still make a purchase within their community. I was looking for a specific Ashanti antelope woodcarving and had explored one vendor stall after another, never finding exactly what I was looking for. "Mama," they called to me, as a series of vendors questioned me and brought their merchandise until they found what I was looking for in the stall of one of their colleagues. The extended family is the foundation of society.

The men, women and children own an appearance and mannerism of confidence and pride in their eyes; their walk and speech as they hustled to earn a living, cared for their children and maintained their homes. The people are very clean, although many sidewalks and streets were not paved, but covered with the red clay earth; sanitation and trash pick-up was next to nil; and, indoor plumbing and underground sewage was almost non-existent. Driving through one village, we passed a yard full of perfectly bright fresh laundry of white sheets and clothing bellowing in the breeze like a winter white sail gliding over a calm lake. Even in such conditions, the laundry looked better than mine and I use Tide and Clorox! As I continued to explore the towns and villages I saw men and women in front of their homes, vendors' stalls and other places of business sweeping the African soil of trash to keep their personal environment tidy and clean.

What Happened?

Why have we stopped supporting each
another and respecting ourselves?

Why do we tolerate liquors stores on every
other corner in our communities?

How many of us actually vote, volunteer our
time to community, visit the sick, feed the
hungry and help the homeless?

Our abundance is poured into fancy clothes,
expensive cars and electronic tinker toys that
close out the world around us.

We move to the suburbs instead of using
our tax dollars to support the inner cities.
If we weren't born with a keener nose and
long blond hair, we buy it.
We mortgage our homes to support the
mega-churches with overflowing congregations
housing empty souls. We degrade our mothers and
daughters through music and media.

Willie Lynch did an outstanding job destroying
our commitment to family and community.

Regain our strength!
Know that we come from
an industrious, communal, salient, striking,
artistic, kindhearted linage.

Reinforce our strength!
Rethink our priorities, educate and support
our youth, sustain our families.

Renew our spirits!
Love ourselves so we can love one another.

Restore our strength!
It can only get better.

A Letter to My Grandchildren

January 20, 2009

Dear Yasmin, Ezekiel, Erin and Paiten:

The purpose of this letter is to document and share with you the overwhelming joy, relief and sense of accomplishment in history that I witnessed TODAY…CHANGE came to America and the world. I just returned from the inauguration of the 44th President of the United States, Barack Hussein Obama. I am aching from head to toe but, I was there. Today is the epitome of American history past, present or future. There will never be anything that could surpass the American people's election of the first African-American President! Many thought we'd never live to see this day. It was surreal to be present and witness "OUR" new President take the oath of office to defend, represent and improve the conditions of this country and our relationship with the world. A man who exemplifies brilliance, fortitude, focus, faith and a sincere desire to make this a better world, while ALWAYS with an attitude of Humility! As one "white" person in the crowd shouted, "We now have our country back!"

Your Uncle Wright, Cousin Sheila and I had tickets to the official inaugural swearing-in ceremony at the U.S. Capital. We left the house, still dark at 5:30 in the morning, below freezing temperature, prepared to walk, be cold and hungry; whatever it took we were going to be there. Happy and filled with high expectations, we caught the bus downtown. People traveled from all over the country. As we traveled down Georgia Avenue, the bus was buzzing with excitement. We disembarked in Chinatown, at 7th and H Streets, Northwest, met by hundreds of people; every race, accent, old and young, man, woman and child energized and going in the same direction. We were headed to the Mall to see America fulfill the Constitutional promise that all people are equal. Everyone was smiling and talking to each other, many wearing Obama memorabilia. Vendors were on both sides of the streets selling everything imaginable. People from every corner of the United States and from all over the world were making their way to the Mall. Some walked, some traveled the Metro and some rode the bus. The atmosphere was exploding with energy as we tried to find our designated entry point.

We must have walked over four miles in circles, maybe two hours for a journey that should not have taken more than a mile or 30 minutes, tops. After experiencing several bottleneck crowds, receiving misguided directions and your Uncle Wright's domineering approach we finally made it through our security checkpoint into the silver ticket holder's area.

There were approximately two million people on the Mall, extending from the steps of the Capital to the Lincoln Memorial and beyond. I experienced a sea of love and anticipation. People were shoulder to shoulder as far as the eye could see; the rich and poor, the famous and not so famous—there was no respect of person in the crowd. Some had been there since 2:00 a.m. We were cold, moving against strong winds. My lips felt like they had been injected with Novocain. Nevertheless, ignoring the chills the band played, we cheered with enthusiasm, waving small flags often shouting, "O-bama, O-bama, O-bama;" or "give me an O, give me a B, give me an A, give me an M, give me an A... Obama!" There were big screens strategically placed so we could see and hear everything. We even shouted, "Yes We Can, Yes We Can," during his speech. Every time he, or Michelle or the daughters appeared on the big screen the crowd erupted into loud applauses of approval and gratitude. The spirit was high, the feelings were warm, and the expectation of the new President was intoxicating …love, laughter and hugs everywhere.

The most profound moment for me was when President-elect Obama was walking down the stairs just prior to being announced to enter the podium. A brief moment alone, he had the most solemn, humble, almost fearful expression on his face, as if to say, "Lord, what have I gotten myself into?" He looked like he was being taken to his own crucifixion. I got goose bumps, wanting to carry some of the weight that is now on his shoulders. But, when he walked through the doors facing his American public he expressed the same self-confidence and humility he had always shown throughout his campaign. You could sense everyone's hope when Barack Obama raised his right hand with his wife, Michelle, by his side, both exuding confidence, pride and humility. At 12:05 p.m. "... So help me God," Barack Obama said, as he finished the oath of office to become the 44th President of these United States! Yes, I saw it all and like many others there were tears streaming down our cheeks as we embraced with unprecedented hope in our hearts.

Everyone's walk home was longer and harder than the morning. Sheila and I walked from the Capital building to the Arlington Cemetery Metro to catch the train home. Uncle Wright walked from the Capital to the Navy Yard metro and your Uncle Eric walked from the Monument to the Waterfront metro. I fell once, body aching from head to toe, but I did not stop. The walk was representative of the difficult painful journey endured for more than 400 years by our ancestors who fought for deserved equality and success in America. It was achieved today. Equally important, our long and painful journey home was also representative of what our great nation will face to reclaim its integrity, wealth, global goodwill and creditability. Again, we cannot stop. The difference is ALL Americans are now willing to work and march forward together.

In closing, the history books will document the greatness of the man, the profound CHANGE expected for our nation that he promoted and promised; and, his mantra of integrity, responsibility and accountability that must be assumed by all. To that end, know that God doesn't bless you by yourself, but what He gives you give to others; what He does for you do for others. Also know you can achieve your dreams—the door has been opened!

Yasmin, Zeke, Erin, and Paiten. I intended to tell you what I saw, heard and felt today, but could not help reflecting on the magnitude of the moment. I hope I succeeded.

The world rejoiced today! The world was reminded of the vision of Martin Luther King, Jr. today! The world was reunited today! CHANGE came to America, today!

I love you dearly.

Mantra

I am a beautifully and wonderfully made Child of God.
I am emotionally, physically and spiritually well.
I "accept" only what is good and pure and true into my life.
I "give" only what is good and pure and true.
I am graceful and grateful.

I receive _____ into my life, NOW!

Insert your desires

Joy
Peace
Power
Prosperity
Health
Success
Love
Happiness

Earnell Brown is an author and international traveler who was born and raised in the Trinidad community of Washington, DC. Ironically, she later lived and worked for five years in Trinidad, West Indies.

Her journeys have taken her across the continents of Africa, Asia, Europe, North America and South America, but she especially loves the Caribbean, snorkeling, its beaches, and savoring its sunsets.

The sights, sounds, smells, and people encountered on her travels inspired many of the poems and essays in Earnell's first book of poetry, *I've Been Where I'm Going*. Her previously published works include the 1998, 1999 and 2008 editions of the *Heritage Black History Calendar*, which integrated early African history with the African-American experience. Each month presented African history, African proverbs, and positive affirmations through scripture.

Earnell is a retired United States Government Internal Revenue Service employee. She ended her career as the IRS Section Head with the U.S. Embassy in Port of Spain, Republic of Trinidad and Tobago (T&T) as the management consultant to the T&T Ministry of Finance.

She was also the first African-American female Division Information Officer in the IRS.

The creative, visionary side of Earnell is expressed in her jewelry designs, watercolor paintings and artistic interior designs. She is a novice golfer and enjoys reading inspirational books as well as fiction and autobiographies. She is an entrepreneur with an extensive volunteer and community service background, and is the mother of three adult children and four delightful grandchildren. Most importantly, she is a child of God and loves the Lord.

Visit Earnell Brown online at www.travelerstreepublishing.com.

LaVergne, TN USA
31 August 2010
195340LV00002B/2/P